The People of
Africa
and Their Food

by Ann L. Burckhardt

C A P S T O N E   P R E S S

M A N K A T O ,   M I N N E S O T A

C A P S T O N E   P R E S S

818 North Willow Street • Mankato, Minnesota 56001

Printed in the United States of America.

Library of Congress Cataloging-in-Publication Data
Burckhardt, Ann, 1933-
        The people of Africa and their food / by Ann L. Burckhardt
        p. cm. -- (Multicultural cookbooks)
    Includes bibliographical references and index.
        ISBN 1-56065-434-1
    1. Cookery, African--Juvenile literature. 2. Food habits--Africa--Juvenile literature. 3. Africa--Social life and customs--Juvenile literature. I. Title. II. Series.
        TX725.A4B87   1996
        641.596--dc20   96-25943
                                                              CIP
                                                              AC

Photo credits
Linda Rother, cover.
Stokka Productions, cover inset, 18, 24, 28, 34, 42.
FPG, 4, 10, 12, 14, 16, 22, 40.
Betty Crowell, 6.
International Stock, 38.

Lisa Fechter, food stylist
Carla Chesley, chef
Cover dish: Jollof rice
Props: Pier 1 Imports

Table of Contents

Fast Facts about Africa

Location: Bounded by the Atlantic Ocean on the west, the Mediterranean Sea on the north, and the Indian Ocean on the east. Europe lies to the north.

Size: 11.7 million square miles (30.4 million square kilometers)

Population: 701 million

Languages: More than 800 native languages plus English, French, German, Portuguese, and Indian languages

Religion: Islam, Christianity, and traditional religions

Climate: Mainly tropical

The pyramids of Egypt are more than 4,000 years old.

Chapter 1

The Countries

The continent of Africa is big. It is the second largest in the world. Only Asia is larger and has more people.

There are more than 50 independent countries in Africa. Some of the nations are very small and some are large. Until the 1940s, most of Africa was ruled by European countries. The African nations have since become independent.

Africa's population is more than 700 million people. African people are divided into 800 different ethnic groups. They have their own languages and customs.The countries with the most people are Nigeria, Egypt, Ethiopia, Zaire, and South Africa.

The huge Sahara Desert covers the top one-third of Africa. It is the biggest desert in the world.

Africa is home to giraffes and other wild animals.

Spain

Mediterranean Sea

Algiers

Casablanca

Atlas Mountains

Sahara Desert

Ahaggar Mountains

Tibesti Mountains

Alexandria

Cairo

Saudi Arabia

Nile River

Red Sea

Niger River

Lagos

Atlantic Ocean

Addis Ababa

N
W E
S

Congo River

Kinshasa

Lake Victoria

Nairobi

Mount Kilimanjaro

Indian Ocean

Lake Nyasa

Madagascar

Namib Desert

Zambezi River

Kalahari Desert

Johannesburg

Cape Town

Drakensberg Mts

The beauty of Africa brings many visitors. People come to see fantastic animals in the wild. They can see elephants, giraffes, lions, tigers, leopards, rhinoceroses, zebras, gazelles, and wildebeests. They can view gorillas, chimps, monkeys, crocodiles, hippos, and many birds.

Other people visit Africa to view its many wonders. They might visit the pyramids in Egypt or Mount Kilimanjaro in Tanzania.

Africa's deserts, mountains, and rain forests influence what the people cook and eat. Climate and geography play a big role in the types of crops and livestock that are raised. The food and cooking customs are varied.

In West Africa, for example, peanuts are a major crop. Peanut soup is a common meal.

In South Africa, the large East Indian community has influenced the cooking. Indian curry is very popular.

North Africa lies on the Mediterranean Sea and is close to the Middle East. It is influenced by Arab cooking. Many North African dishes contain a tiny grain called couscous (koos-koos).

Chapter 2
The Market

A visit to the market is both a social and an economic activity for many Africans. Shoppers go to open-air markets not only to buy fresh food, but also to see their friends.

Vendors in brightly patterned robes sell green bananas, orange citrus, tan root vegetables, and brown beans. People laugh and talk. Music may be playing. Children selling snacks move among the shoppers.

There are many markets in a city like Nairobi, the capital of Kenya. The 3 million people who live there require a lot of food. Wealthy people shop in modern grocery stores. But most African shoppers take a basket or a shopping bag and go to the nearest open-air market.

A market in Kenya is filled with goods for sale.

There may be as many as 50 to 100 vendors in one place. Some pile their goods in huts. But most simply spread their wares on the ground. Bargaining is the rule. For example, if you want to buy coconuts, stop at several stalls to check their size. Shake them to hear the milk swish inside. Offer a lower price than the one the vendor gives. Soon you can meet halfway on price.

Other vendors go door-to-door selling produce. This is convenient for the elderly and mothers with babies. They find it hard to leave the house.

About two-thirds of Africa's people live in the country. Many families live in remote villages. They go to market to sell what they raise. They also grow the crops and raise the animals that they need themselves. Goat and chicken are common meats. Africans produce most of the world's supply of cocoa beans, yams, and a starchy root called cassava.

Children often have their own garden plots. They work them with their family. Farming in some parts of Africa is difficult. The soil is hard or dry. Many farmers work with hand tools instead of tractors.

A villager carries water in Sudan.

Chapter 3

A Celebration

Kwanzaa is a special holiday that celebrates African culture. Blacks all over the world celebrate the holiday.

It is held for seven days, from December 26 to January 1. It was started in 1966 by an African American. Dr. Maulana Karenga saw that African Americans needed to renew their cultural ways. He wanted African Americans to be proud of their African heritage.

Kwanzaa means "first" in Swahili, a language of East Africa. Its full meaning is "first fruits of the harvest."

There is a theme or principle for each of the seven days of Kwanzaa. A principle is a rule or

A costumed Kenyan prepares to dance.

an important truth. The principles are written in Swahili. They are:

1. Umoja (oo-moh-jah), which means unity.
2. Kujichagulia (koo-gee-cha-goo-lee-yah), which means self-determination.
3. Ujima (oo-gee-mah), which means collective work and responsibility.
4. Ujamaa (oo-jah-mah), which means cooperative economics.
5. Nia (nee-yah), which means purpose in life.
6. Kuumba (koo-oom-bah), which means creativity.
7. Imani (ee-mah-nee), which means faith.

A feast called karamu (kah-rah-moo) is held on the sixth day of Kwanzaa. Family and friends gather for a festive meal.

Everyone brings food, including such traditional African dishes as jollof rice. The recipes in this book would make good additions to a Kwanzaa feast.

Africans take part in a parade in Ivory Coast.

Chapter 4
Main Dishes

African cooks like to prepare entire meals in one pot. This saves on fuel. It also makes it easy to clean up.

Stews may be made with chicken, beef, lamb, or goat. Or they can be made with vegetables.

In West Africa, beef chunks are sold on skewers by street vendors. They also make a great main dish. You can grill them on skewers or broil them.

Chicken is a popular food in Africa. The Jollof Rice combines chicken with rice for a hearty meal.

Jollof rice

Jollof Rice

1 frying chicken, cut into pieces
2 small onions, peeled and cut into chunks
2 green peppers, cut into chunks
2 tablespoons oil
1 cup white rice
1 teaspoon salt
1/2 teaspoon cayenne pepper
1/4 teaspoon dried thyme
14-1/2-ounce can peeled tomatoes
1-3/4 cups water
1 cup frozen mixed vegetables

Rinse and dry chicken. Cut breast pieces in half. Heat the oil in a large pot. Brown chicken pieces in hot oil over medium heat. Remove them from the pan and keep warm in a 250-degree oven.

Add the onion and pepper chunks to the pan. Cook and stir until the onion is yellow. Add the rice. Cook and stir until rice is coated with oil. Season the mixture with salt, cayenne pepper, and thyme. Pour in the tomatoes, water, and frozen vegetables. Stir well.

Place chicken on top of vegetable mixture. Cover and cook 45 minutes, until meat and rice are tender. Check about halfway through. Add more water if rice is sticking to the bottom of the pan. Serves 6.

Spicy Meat Cubes

1 pound round steak, cut into 3/4-inch cubes
1/2 cup dry-roasted peanuts
1/2 teaspoon ground ginger
1/2 teaspoon salt
1/4 teaspoon cayenne pepper
1/8 teaspoon paprika

Start heating the oven so that it can be used for broiling. Put dry-roasted peanuts into a plastic bag. Use a rolling pin or the smooth side of a meat mallet to crush the peanuts. Add the ginger, salt, cayenne pepper, and paprika to the bag.

Shake bag well to mix the seasonings. Put about one-third of the meat cubes in the bag. Shake well to coat meat on all sides. Remove meat from bag. Repeat to coat all the meat.

Spray the broiling rack with nonstick spray or rub with shortening. Arrange the cubes on the broiling rack. Put them on skewers, if you like. Broil cubes 3 minutes, turn them over, and broil 3 more minutes. Cubes can be fried in a little oil rather than broiled. Makes four main-dish servings or eight snacks.

Peanut Butter Stew

1-1/2 pound beef chuck or boneless chicken
1 medium onion, cut in rings
1 green pepper, cut in rings
2 tablespoons oil
6-ounce can tomato paste
3/4 cup peanut butter
3 cups water or broth
1 teaspoon salt
1 teaspoon chili powder or 1 teaspoon cayenne pepper
2 cups cooked white rice
Toppings: banana and orange slices, coconut, chopped
    peanuts, hard-boiled eggs, green pepper, tomato

Cut beef or chicken into small pieces. Heat oil in a Dutch oven. Brown the meat on all sides. Remove from pan and set aside. Add onion and pepper rings to the pan. Cook until onion is yellow.

Stir the tomato paste and peanut butter together in a bowl. Add water or broth, salt, and chili powder or cayenne pepper. Stir until mixture is smooth. Add to the vegetables in pan. Add browned meat. Bring mixture to a boil and simmer 20 minutes.

Serve the stew over the rice. Sprinkle with two or three toppings. Serves 6.

A woman stands with a child in Namibia.

Chapter 5

Side Dishes

Separate side dishes, like salads, cooked vegetables, and grains, are rare in Africa. African cooks often stretch their ingredients by cooking meat and vegetables in the same pot.

They sometimes serve a bowl of chopped vegetables to stir into hot food to make it cool.

Leafy greens are popular in Africa. Greens from turnips, beets, carrots, and wild plants are picked when they are young and tender. Africans also eat cabbage, Chinese cabbage, kale, mustard greens, spinach, and Swiss chard.

Steamed greens

Three-in-one Vegetable from Kenya

3 cups instant mashed potatoes, cooked
15-ounce can green peas, drained
15-ounce can whole kernel corn, drained
2 tablespoons butter or margarine
1 teaspoon salt
1/8 teaspoon pepper

Cook instant mashed potatoes as directed on package. With a wooden spoon, push the peas through a sieve to make a thin paste. You may have to repeat this step. Stir the peas into the mashed potatoes.

Stir the corn into the pea-potato mixture. Heat and stir. Season with butter or margarine, salt, and pepper.

The mixture should be stiff enough to form a mound or nest on the plate. Serves 6.

Kitchen smarts: Make a nest of this vegetable mixture. Serve stew in the center.

Steamed Greens from Malawi

10-ounce package frozen chopped spinach
1 medium tomato, chopped
1 tablespoon vegetable oil
pinch of salt

Thaw and drain the chopped spinach. Heat the oil in a small pan. Add spinach. Put on the lid. Keep the pan over medium-high heat. Shake the pan continuously for 4 minutes. Add tomatoes and salt.

Cover the pan again. Cook one or two minutes to heat the tomatoes and blend the flavors. Serves 4.

Chapter 6
Soup and Salad

African cooks make many mixtures in big pots. Sometimes they are thin like a soup. Other times they are thick like a stew. The thickness might depend on how many people will be eating the meal. Or it might depend on the amount of food on hand.

Corn Soup comes from South Africa where it is made from a cornlike grain called mealie. It is similar to North American corn chowder.

The combination of coconut and beans in Kidney Bean Soup comes from Tanzania. Beans like this are called pulses. They are important in the African diet.

Fruit salad

Kidney Bean and Coconut Milk Soup

1/2 cup chopped onions
1/2 cup chopped green pepper
3 tablespoons butter, margarine, or oil
2 teaspoons curry powder
1 cup fresh tomato, cut up
16-ounce can kidney beans, drained
16-ounce can coconut milk
2 cups water
3/4 cup cooked rice
salt and pepper
shredded coconut

Heat butter, margarine, or oil in a soup kettle. Add onion, green pepper, and curry powder. Cook until onion and green pepper are soft.

Add tomato and cook a little longer. Next, add kidney beans, coconut milk, and water. Cook over low heat 10 to 15 minutes. Stir in cooked rice. Cook over low heat until hot. Add salt and pepper to taste. Top with a little shredded coconut when you serve the soup. Serves 8.

Homemade Coconut Milk

2 cups packaged grated coconut
2 cups boiling water

Put coconut in a bowl. Pour the boiling water over it. Let mixture stand for two hours. Strain through a fine sieve, pressing with a spoon to push out all the milk.

You can repeat this process to make a second batch of coconut milk. Any milk not used should be covered and refrigerated.

Corn Soup with Tomato

1 cup chopped onion
3 tablespoons butter, margarine, or oil
1 cup fresh tomatoes, cut up
15-ounce can cream-style corn
15-ounce can whole kernel corn, drained
12-ounce can evaporated milk
3 cups chicken broth
pepper

Heat butter, margarine, or oil in large pan. Add onion and cook until soft. Add the tomatoes. Cook 5 minutes. Add cream-style corn, whole kernel corn, evaporated milk, chicken broth, and pepper to taste.

Cover the soup and cook over low heat about 15 minutes. Serves 6.

Kitchen smarts: The soup recipe does not call for salt because chicken broth is usually quite salty. This soup would be a good food to put in a thermos bottle to eat for lunch.

Fruit Salad

2 cups watermelon or cantaloupe, cut up
2 oranges, cut up
2 tangerines, cut up
1 apple, peeled and sliced
15-ounce can tropical fruit salad, drained
15-ounce can pineapple chunks, drained
2 bananas, sliced
3 tablespoons lemon juice
shredded coconut
chopped peanuts

Put canned fruit and all fresh fruit, except bananas, in a scrving bowl. Toss fruit gently using two spoons. Add bananas and lemon juice. Toss again.

Sprinkle with shredded coconut or chopped peanuts or both. Serves 10.

Kitchen smarts: Lemon juice keeps the apple and bananas from darkening.

Chapter 7

Dessert and Beverages

Fresh fruit is abundant in Africa. Diners can choose from mangoes, bananas, dates, passion fruit, oranges, limes, papaya, and many kinds of melons.

Ginger is popular in Africa. You can enjoy its taste in gingerbread and ginger root beer. The root beer will satisfy your thirst during hot weather. The ginger root gives it a real kick.

A tea-based milk drink is popular in East Africa and India. It is called Railway Tea. Travelers drink it to stay awake during long train trips. It is served with bread and cookies.

Upside-down banana gingerbread and coconut milk

Upside-Down Banana Gingerbread

2-1/2 small bananas, sliced
1 package gingerbread mix

Preheat the oven to 350 degrees. Grease a 9-inch square baking pan. Arrange banana slices to cover the bottom of the pan in a single layer. Prepare gingerbread mix according to package directions.

Pour the batter over the banana slices. Smooth the batter with the back of a spoon. Bake the cake 35 to 40 minutes. Cake is done when it starts to pull away from the sides of the pan and when the top of the cake bounces back if you touch it lightly with your finger.

Cool cake about 5 minutes. Loosen the cake from the pan by running a knife around the edge. Put a dinner plate upside down over the pan. Take a hot pad in each hand. Hold the plate and pan together. Flip them over so the plate with the cake on it is on the bottom. Serve with whipped cream or ice cream. Serves 6.

Ginger Root Beer

1/2 pound fresh ginger root
3 cups water
1/2 cup lemon juice
1/3 cup sugar

Break the fresh ginger root into chunks. Using a vegetable peeler, peel off as much of the brown skin as you can get off easily. Slice the ginger root into thin slices, about 1/8-inch thick.

Put ginger root in a medium pan with the water. Bring to a boil. Cover pan, reduce heat, and cook over low heat about 20 minutes. Pour the ginger water into a bowl. Throw away the root. Add lemon juice and sugar to the ginger water.

Stir until sugar is dissolved. Pour into a quart jar and cover with a lid. This is the root beer base. Refrigerate until ready to serve.

To serve: Fill a glass one-third to one-half full with root beer base. Add an ice cube. Then fill with very cold water. Makes 10 glasses.

Kitchen smarts: Decorate the glasses this way. Dip the rim of a glass in water. Next dip it in sugar. Put the glass in the freezer for a short time until the sugar sets.

Railway Tea

2 cups water
1 or 2 cinnamon sticks, broken into pieces
3 cardamom pods, cracked open
2 tablespoons loose black tea
2 cups whole milk
1/4 cup sugar

Bring water to boil in a medium pan. Stir in black tea, cinnamon pieces, and cracked cardamom, an Indian spice. Remove from heat 5 to 10 minutes. The longer it stands the stronger it will be. This is called steeping the tea.

Put pan back on heat. Pour in milk. Heat the mixture until you can see steam coming from the surface. Stir occasionally. Do not let the mixture start to boil. Stir in sugar. Makes 1 quart.

Kitchen smarts: Extra tea should be kept in the refrigerator. It is very good reheated. For a thicker drink, use evaporated milk. That is what they use in East Africa.

Tea is served at a hotel in Casablanca, Morocco.

Metric Measurements Chart

Use the chart below to convert recipe amounts in standard units to metric units.

Volume

1 teaspoon = 5 milliliters
1 tablespoon = 15 milliliters
1 fluid ounce = 30 milliliters
1 cup = 0.24 liter
1 pint = 0.47 liter
1 quart = 0.95 liter
(to convert liters to quarts, multiply by 1.06)

Weight

1 ounce = 28 grams
1 pound = 0.45 kilogram
2.2 pounds = 1 kilogram
(to convert grams to ounces, multiply by .035)

Fresh fish is sold at a market in Lagos, Nigeria.

Kitchen Safety

Here are some guidelines for cooking success.

1. Before cooking, read through the entire recipe. Make sure you understand each step. Clear your work space of odds and ends. Turn off the radio and television. Then you can concentrate.

2. Get out all the ingredients and equipment that you will need. Then, if something is missing, you can find a substitute.

3. Wash your hands completely before you start and as needed while cooking. Do not forget the backs of your hands and the spaces between your fingers. Always wash the fruits and vegetables you will be preparing, too.

4. You work best and safest when the work space is at the right height. You might need to stand on a stool for the best arm motion while cutting or stirring.

Get out all the equipment you need before starting to cook.

5. Sharp knives and peelers require respect. Ask someone older to give you a hand with cutting, chopping, and slicing. Remember to move the peeler away from yourself. Always use a clean cutting board.

6. Protect yourself from burns. Always use a hot pad or mitt with hot pans. Turn the handles of pots and pans to the back of the range. Then you will not bump into them. Keep baking soda or salt close by to sprinkle on the flames if something catches fire. Never put water on a grease fire.

7. Try to clean up as you cook. If you have to wait for something to boil or bake, use that time to wash bowls and pans. Then put things away. Those who share your kitchen will thank you.

Cooking Glossary

boil—to heat a liquid over high heat until bubbles form and rise rapidly to the surface

broil—to cook close to direct heat

Dutch oven—a heavy iron pot with a tight-fitting cover

grate—to cut food into tiny pieces using a special utensil

preheat—to allow an oven to reach the desired baking temperature before use

produce—fresh fruits and vegetables

shred   to tear or cut into small pieces

sieve—a device with holes in it, used for draining liquid from food

thaw—to allow frozen food to reach room temperature

To Learn More

Ayo, Yvonne. *Africa.* New York: Alfred A. Knopf, 1995.

Gibrill, Martin. *African Food and Drink.* New York: The Bookwright Press, 1989.

Harris, Colin. *A Taste of West Africa.* New York: Thomson Learning, 1994.

Nabwire, Constance and Bertha Vining Montgomery. *Cooking the African Way.* Minneapolis: Lerner Publications, 1988.

Useful Addresses and Internet Sites

African Studies Association
Emory University
Credit Union Building
Atlanta, GA 30322

World Learning
P.O. Box 676
Brattleboro, VT 05302-0676

The African Cookbook
http://www.sas.upenn.edu/African_Studies/Cookbook/about_cb_wh.html

African Links on the Internet
http://www.cis.yale.edu/swahili/afrilink.html

The Global Gastronomer—Cuisines of the World
http://www.cs.yale.edu/homes/hupfer/global/gastronomer.html

K-12 Africa Guide
http://www.sas.upenn.edu/African_Studies/home_Page/AFR_GIDE.html

Index